Why Is the Grass Green?

A **Just Ask** Book

Hi, my name is Christopher!

by Chris Arvetis
and Carole Palmer

illustrated by James Buckley

Copyright © 1985 by Rand McNally & Company
All rights reserved
Printed in Italy
Library of Congress Catalog Card Number: 85-60558

CHILDRENS PRESS CHOICE

A Rand McNally title selected for educational distribution

ISBN 0-516-09808-X

1985 SCHOOL AND LIBRARY EDITION

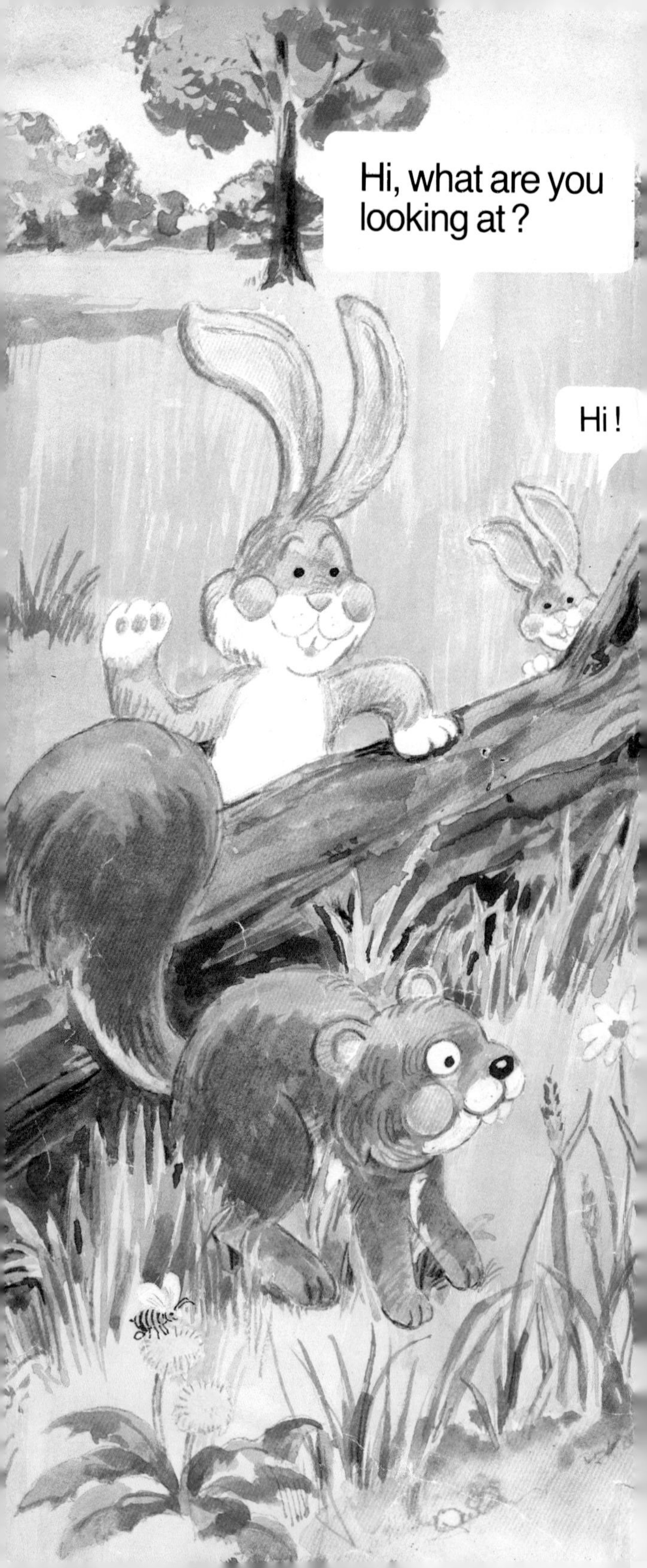
Hi, what are you looking at?
Hi!

I'm looking at the grass. Look how green it is. Every little piece is green.

It certainly is!

I wonder why.
Can you tell me—
why is the grass
green?

I have no idea.
Maybe our friend
the cow can tell us.

She'll know!

She nibbles on the
grass all day!

Mrs. Cow, do you know anything about grass? Can you tell us– why is it green?

Well, Christopher, stop and look around you. It's not just the grass that's green. Almost all the plants here are green.
I never knew that!

And the plants all
have leaves.

But the leaves look
different from each other.

They come in many
shapes and sizes.

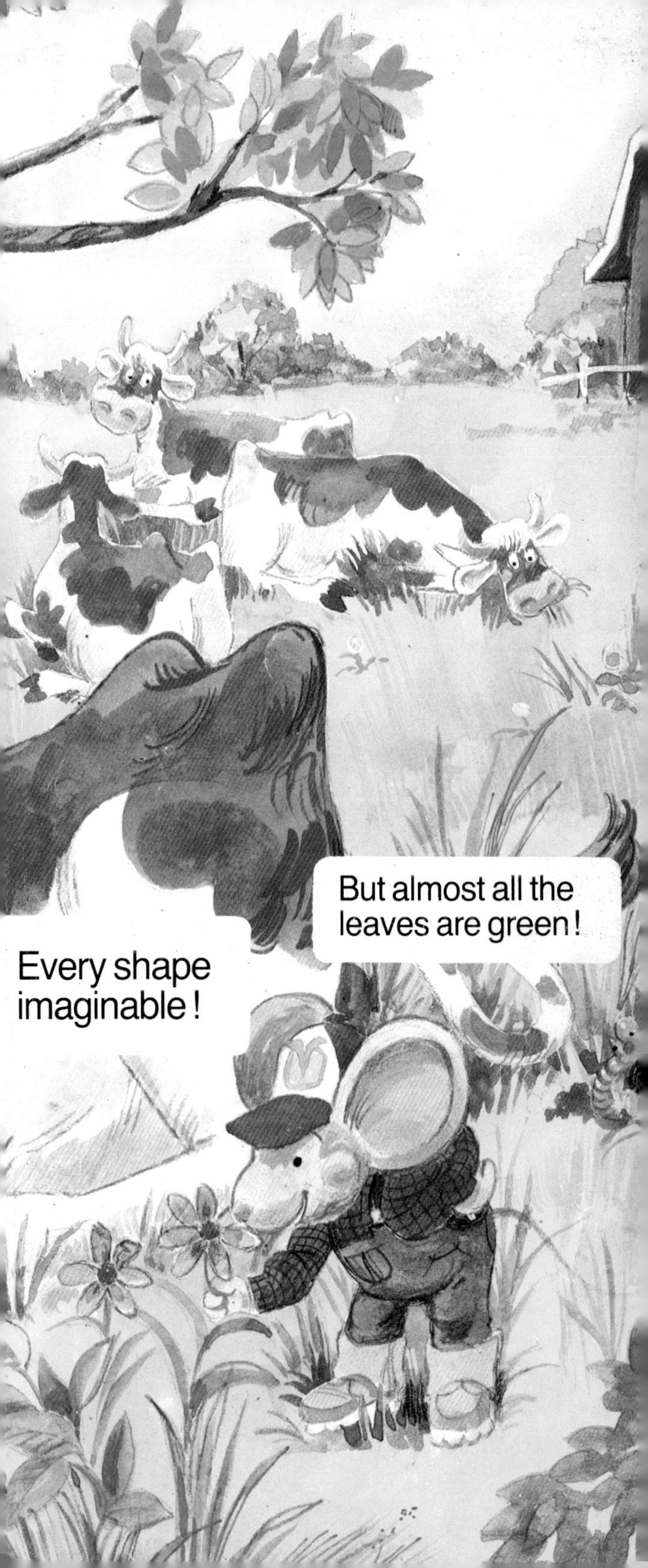
But almost all the leaves are green!
Every shape imaginable!

Let's find out
about leaves.
Look at that little bud,
Christopher.
It is the beginning
of a tiny leaf.

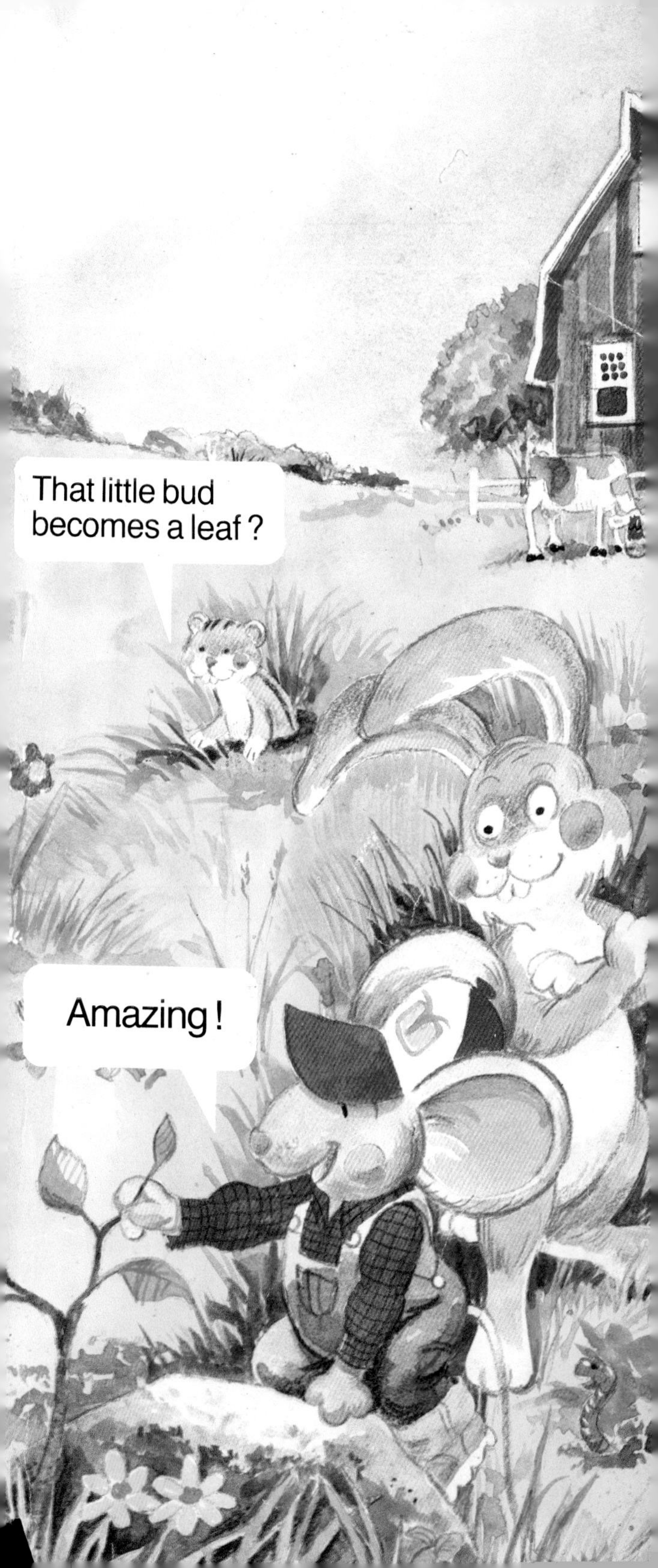
That little bud becomes a leaf ?
Amazing !

As the sun warms the bud,
the leaf starts to grow
The leaf has many parts
we can't see with our eyes.
Let's look at a drawing.
It will help you understand.

Let's pretend we can look inside the leaf.

See the special little green parts?

They contain CHLOROPHYLL.

Say CHLO-RO-PHYLL with me.

CHLO-RO-PHYLL!

The leaf needs chlorophyll.
The leaf uses the chlorophyll to help make a special food for the whole plant.
Let's see what else the leaf needs.

Mmm, tastes good!

The leaf needs sunlight.
It gets light and energy
from the sun.

The warm sun
feels good !

The leaf needs water.
The plant's roots bring
water to the leaf.

The leaf also needs
carbon dioxide.
We can't see carbon dioxide,
but it is a gas in the air.
The green chlorophyll is
very important.
It takes in the sunlight
that makes the whole
plant grow.
Let's see how…

I can't see it!

You can't see it!

Can you?

It's in the air!

Each leaf is like a tiny little factory that makes a special food for the plant.

The factory uses sunlight, water, carbon dioxide and chlorophyll.

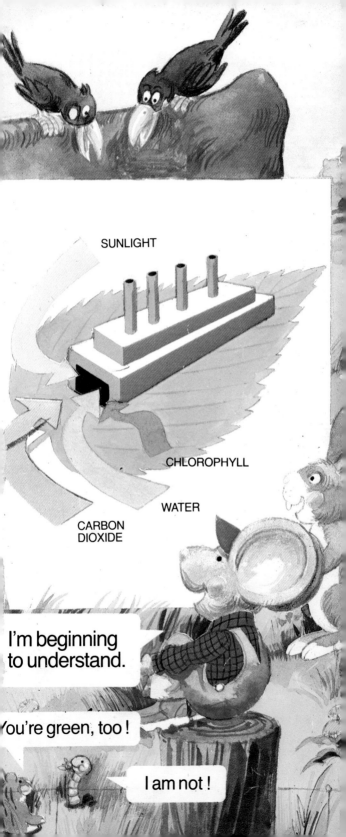

SUNLIGHT

The way the plant makes
food is called
PHOTOSYNTHESIS.
That's a gigantic word!

PHO-TO-SYN-THE-SIS !

CHLOROPHYLL

ARBON
IOXIDE

WATER

As the plant makes its food,
it gives off another gas
called oxygen.
All of us need oxygen
to live and grow.

I never
knew tha

Now we see how the little leaf factories use the light from the sun, carbon dioxide from the air, water from the roots, and the green chlorophyll in the leaf to make the plant's food.

Photosynthesis is
hard work, but the
little leaf factories
keep the plant healthy
and growing.
And that is why the plant
stays green.

Is that why?

Of course!

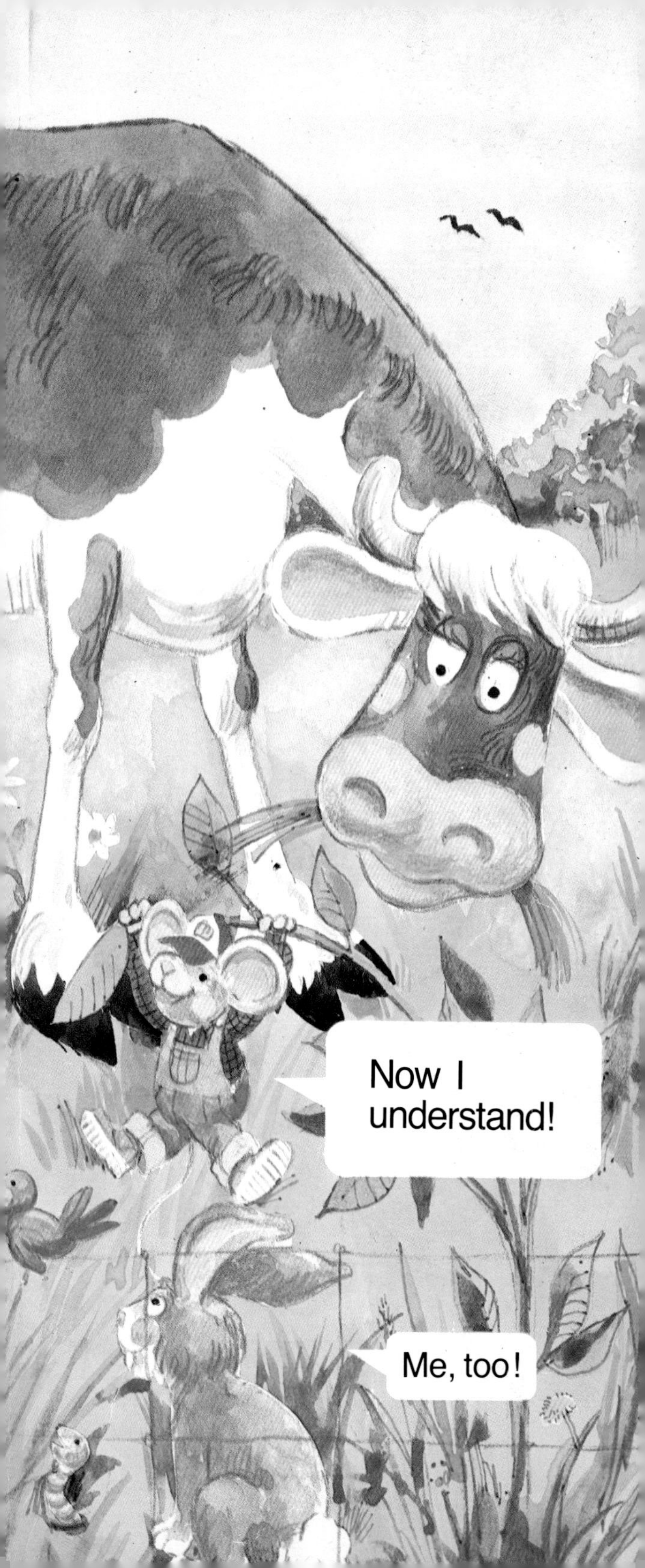
Now I understand!
Me, too!

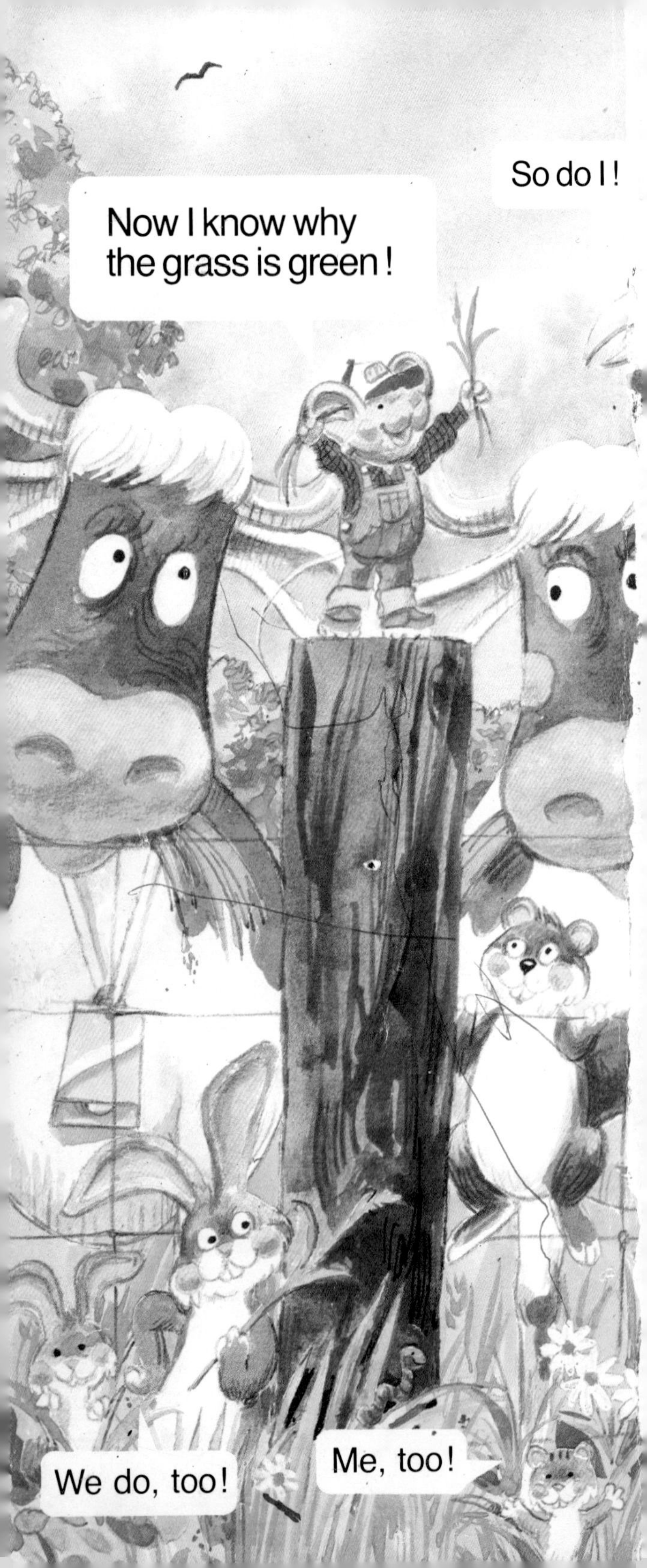

Now I know why the grass is green!
So do I!
We do, too!
Me, too!